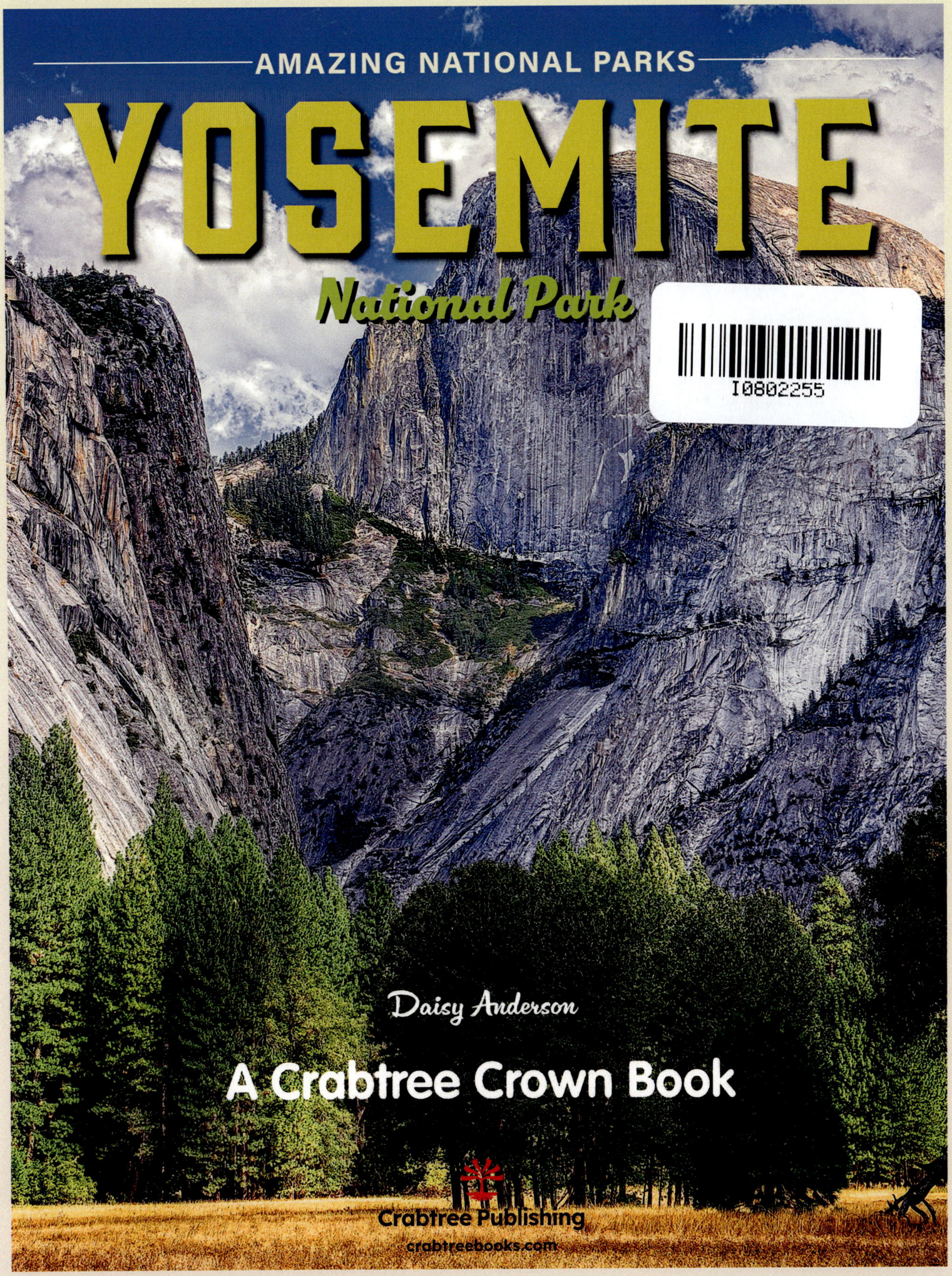

AMAZING NATIONAL PARKS

YOSEMITE

National Park

Daisy Anderson

A Crabtree Crown Book

Crabtree Publishing
crabtreebooks.com

School-to-Home Support for Caregivers and Teachers

This appealing book is designed to teach students about core subject areas. Students will build upon what they already know about the subject, and engage in topics that they want to learn more about. Here are a few guiding questions to help readers build their comprehension skills. Possible answers appear here in red.

Before Reading:

What do I know about Yosemite National Park?

- *I know the national park is in the Sierra Nevada mountain range.*
- *I know many people visit Yosemite National Park.*

What do I want to learn about this topic?

- *I want to learn what people can see in the national park.*
- *I want to learn what people can do in the national park.*

During Reading:

I'm curious to know...

- *I'm curious to know what kinds of animals live in the national park.*
- *I'm curious to know what kinds of plants grow in the national park.*

How is this like something I already know?

- *I know that bears often live in mountains.*
- *I know that some of the trees in the national park are very tall.*

After Reading:

What was the author trying to teach me?

- *The author was trying to teach me about why so many people visit Yosemite National Park.*
- *The author was trying to teach me what visitors can see at the national park.*

How did the photographs and captions help me understand more?

- *The photographs helped me picture what the national park looks like.*
- *The captions gave me extra information about what there is to see at the national park.*

TABLE OF CONTENTS

Chapter 1
WELCOME TO YOSEMITE NATIONAL PARK

Waterfalls spill from towering **cliffs**. These mountains are home to one of the oldest national parks in the United States. Millions of people visit Yosemite National Park every year!

Know the Park

The U.S. government owns national parks and takes care of them. National parks are used to help protect natural areas.

Know the Park

Mount Lyell is the highest mountain in the national park. It stands 13,114 feet (3,997 meters) tall.

Yosemite National Park is in eastern California. It covers 1,169 square miles (3,028 square kilometers) of the Sierra Nevada mountain range. The Sierra Nevada has some of the highest mountains in the U.S.

BEFORE IT WAS A PARK

Native American peoples lived in the area beginning thousands of years ago. In the 1400s, the Ahwahneechee people made their homes in Yosemite Valley. Miners in search of gold and **settlers** who wanted to build homes came to the area in the mid-1800s. They clashed with the Ahwahneechee. Thousands of Ahwahneechee people died in the war that followed.

By the 1860s, Yosemite's beauty began to bring visitors from all over the United States. In 1864, President Abraham Lincoln signed a bill to make it a protected area. The Ahwahneechee continued to live in Yosemite, but their way of life was changing.

Abraham Lincoln

FOUNDING THE PARK

In 1868, **naturalist** John Muir visited Yosemite. Inspired by the beauty of the area, he wanted it to be **preserved** as a national park. He wrote letters and articles about it. The U.S. Congress made it a national park on October 1, 1890.

John Muir

Know the Park

At first, the Ahwahneechee were allowed to stay in their homes and work in the park. Starting in the 1950s, park officials forced them to move. Today no Native Americans live within the national park.

THE PARK TODAY

Yosemite National Park is the 16th-largest national park in the United States. It's also one of the most visited national parks. More than 4 million people enjoy Yosemite National Park every year!

Chapter 2
THE LAND AND CLIMATE

The Sierra Nevada mountains are mostly **granite** rock that formed more than 90 million years ago. Scientists believe the rock was **uplifted** into mountains about 45 million years ago.

The oldest rocks in the park are granite.

Around 3 million years ago, **glaciers** began to change the mountains. Huge amounts of slow-moving ice and snow created wide, U-shaped valleys. Glaciers also rounded rock into **domes**.

Know the Park

To see a U-shaped glacial valley, stop in Yosemite Valley. It's one of the national park's most popular places to visit.

CLIMATE

Yosemite National Park has all four seasons, but much of the area is covered in snow from November to May. Several feet of snow may fall in the mountains during this time. The highest peaks sometimes have snow on the ground as late as July.

Know the Park

Melting snow feeds Yosemite's waterfalls. Waterfall flow is usually at its highest in May as the winter snow melts.

Spring brings warm weather to the national park. Its lower **elevations** may have hot summers. Yosemite Valley sometimes reaches 100 °F (38 °C). It's always colder at the top of the mountains than at the bottom. It might be 50 °F (10 °C) at the peaks but 82 °F (28 °C) in the valleys at the same time.

Chapter 3

PLANTS IN THE PARK

Different plants grow at different elevations in the national park. Green forests of oak and pine trees grow below 8,000 feet (2,438 meters) in the mountains. Yosemite's famous giant sequoias are found there, too. These trees may be more than 200 feet (61 meters) tall.

Know the Park

The national park has three groves of giant sequoias. Mariposa Grove has more than 500 of the massive trees.

The **subalpine** forest begins around 8,000 feet (2,438 meters). This area covers 297,000 acres (120,000 hectares) of the national park. Evergreen trees such as the western white pine grow there. Large, open meadows blanket the ground.

The national park has more than 2,000 lakes.

The **alpine** zone's cold and snowy weather is too harsh for most plants. No trees grow above 9,500 feet (2,900 meters). Only plants that are low to the ground such as grasses and mosses survive there.

FLOWERING PLANTS

Spring brings bursts of color to Yosemite as wildflowers blossom. About 1,450 different kinds of wildflowers grow in the national park. Many bloom between May and June. Flowers higher up in the mountains may not appear until the snow melts in July.

Visitors can see Yosemite Falls, Half Dome, Glacier Point, and Sentinel Rock from Cook's Meadow.

Chapter 4
ANIMALS IN THE PARK

Many animals roam the national park's wilderness. Mule deer munch on plants in valleys and open meadows. Mountain lions hunt deer and smaller animals such as raccoons and coyotes. More than 200 bird **species** have been spotted in Yosemite.

Black-headed grosbeaks spend spring and summer in Yosemite.

Know the Park

It's important that visitors do not feed the bears. Our food is not good for them. Bears may also harm people who come too close.

BLACK BEARS

Between 300 to 500 black bears live in Yosemite. Few actually have black fur—most are brown or even blond. Males weigh around 250 pounds (113 kilograms). Black bears eat grasses, berries, and insects. Grizzly bears once lived in the region, but today there are none left in all of California.

BUTTERFLIES

Around 100 species of butterflies live in Yosemite. They flutter through forests, meadows, and valleys. Some even live at the highest points in the park. Alpine butterflies make their homes in the mountains at 10,000 feet (3,048 meters) and higher.

Know the Park

Male tarantulas travel the national park in the fall to look for mates. Visitors should keep an eye out for them on roads and stop to let the spiders cross safely.

WATCHING WILDLIFE

Yosemite has large animals such as bears, but even a small squirrel can bite. It's important to remember that all the animals in the national park are wild. Keeping your distance and watching through binoculars or by zooming in with your camera is the safest way to enjoy the wildlife.

People have been taking pictures of Yosemite's amazing views since the mid-1800s.

Chapter 5
TIPS ON WHAT TO SEE

Know the Park

Half Dome was once rounded on all sides. Over time, glaciers and weather wore away the rock, creating the steep side that gives Half Dome its name.

HALF DOME

Half Dome is one of the best-known rocks in the park. The top of it stands almost 5,000 feet (1,524 meters) above Yosemite Valley. The hike up to Half Dome is 14 to 16 miles (23 to 26 kilometers) round trip. Thousands do this challenging climb every year.

Know the Park

Yosemite is famous for its many waterfalls. Some can be spotted from the road. Others can only be reached by hiking.

YOSEMITE FALLS

Yosemite Falls is one of the world's tallest waterfalls. It is 2,425 feet (739 meters) from the top to the base. Visitors can take a shuttle bus to a 1-mile (1.6-kilometer) trail that leads to the waterfall's base. The eastern loop of the trail is wheelchair friendly.

Know the Park

Along with El Capitan, visitors can also see Cathedral Rock and Cathedral Spires from El Capitan Meadow.

EL CAPITAN

The Ahwahneechee people first named this rock Tutokanula. It stands more than 3,000 feet (914 meters) above Yosemite Valley. Climbers take from two to six days to reach the top. For one of the best views of El Capitan without climbing, visit El Capitan Meadow in Yosemite Valley.

GLACIER POINT

Glacier Point Road leads to Glacier Point, an overlook with one of Yosemite's best views. Visitors take a short, wheelchair-friendly trail to Glacier Point, which sits 3,214 feet (980 meters) above the valley floor. From there, visitors can see Yosemite Valley, Half Dome, and Yosemite Falls.

Glacier Point Road is closed in the winter months.

Chapter 6
TIPS ON WHAT TO DO

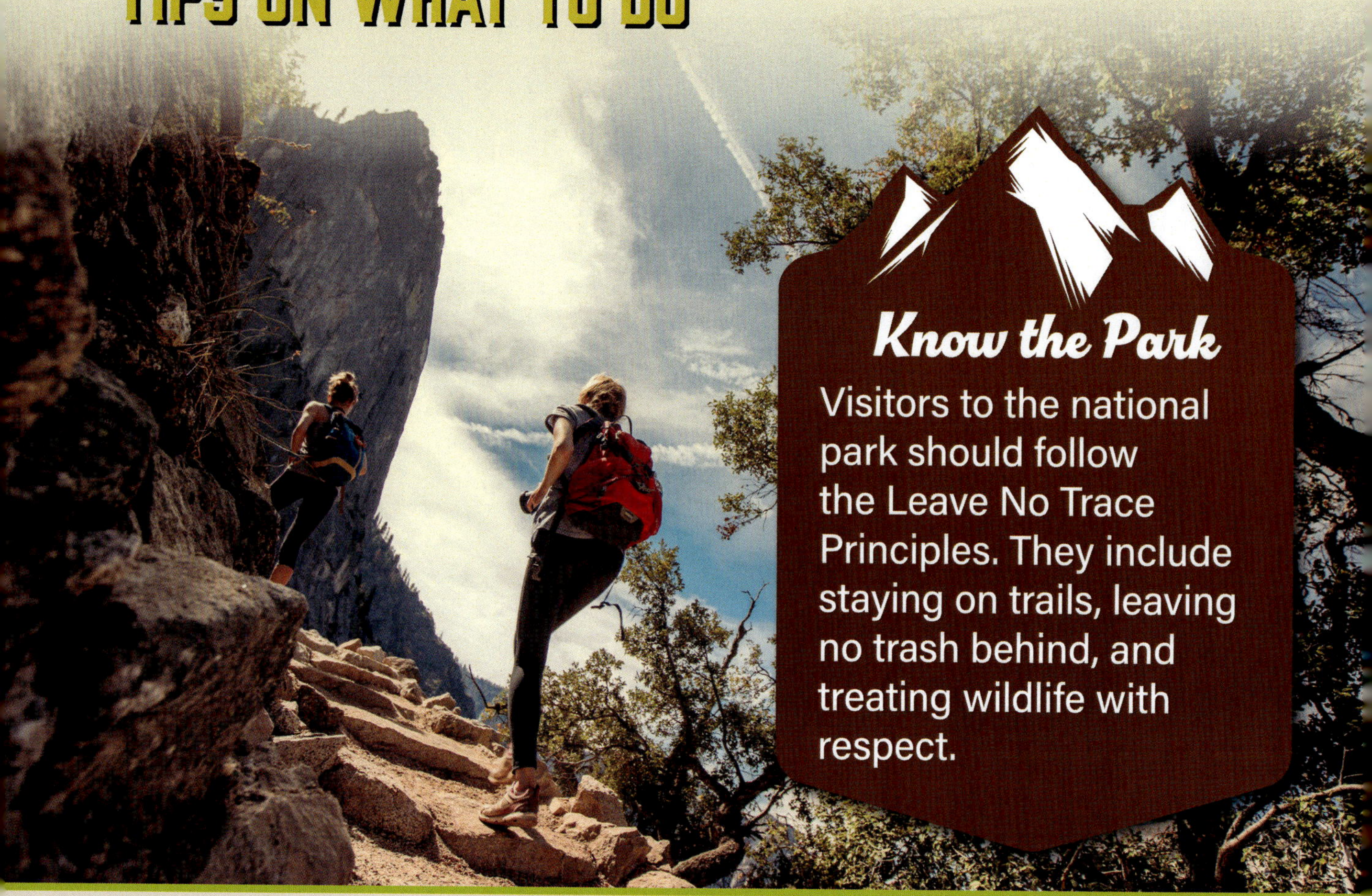

Know the Park

Visitors to the national park should follow the Leave No Trace Principles. They include staying on trails, leaving no trash behind, and treating wildlife with respect.

HIKING

Yosemite has more than 750 miles (1,207 kilometers) of hiking trails. Hikes range from short, easy walks to difficult trails that take hours or even days. Yosemite also has picnic areas for visitors to enjoy.

The national park's campgrounds need reservations from April through October.

CAMPING

Yosemite's 13 campgrounds have something for everyone. Some may be reached by car. The national park also has camps for horseback riders. Backcountry campsites are available for backpackers.

BECOME A JUNIOR RANGER

Kids can become Yosemite Junior Rangers! When kids visit Yosemite National Park and complete activities in the Junior Ranger Handbook, they will receive a badge from a park ranger. The Junior Ranger Handbook can be downloaded or picked up at any Yosemite visitor center.

Kids from ages 4 to 12 may become Yosemite Junior Rangers.

Whether you hike, camp, or become a Junior Ranger, Yosemite National Park is a mountain adventure!

GLOSSARY

alpine (AL-pine): Of or found high in the mountains above the tree line

cliffs (KLIFS): High, steep rock faces

domes (DOHMZ): Curved formations shaped like half a ball

elevation (el-uh-VAY-shun): The height of a place above sea level

glaciers (GLAY-shurz): Giant masses of ice and snow that move like very slow rivers

granite (GRAN-it): A very hard type of rock that is often gray but may also be pink, white, or black

naturalist (NACH-ur-uh-list): A person who studies the natural world, including plants and animals

preserve (pri-ZURV): To protect something so that it stays in its original state

settlers (SET-lers): People who move to a new place and make it their home

species (SPEE-seez): A group of animals or plants that are similar and can reproduce with one another

subalpine (SUB-al-pine): Of or found in the mountains just below the tree line

uplift (UHP-lift): An increase in the vertical elevation of Earth's surface as a result of natural causes

INDEX

COMPREHENSION QUESTIONS

1. Yosemite National Park is in ____.
   a. Colorado
   b. Utah
   c. California
2. Yosemite is famous for its many ____.
   a. canyons
   b. waterfalls
   c. rivers
3. The highest peaks in Yosemite may have snow on the ground as late as ____.
   a. August
   b. October
   c. July
4. True or False: Yosemite National Park is in the Sierra Nevada mountain range.
5. True or False: Grizzly bears live in the national park.

Answers: 1. C, 2. B, 3. C, 4. True, 5. False

ABOUT THE AUTHOR

Daisy Anderson loves to write real-life books for curious kids. She lives in the Midwest, where she enjoys exploring the great outdoors with her two dogs. When Daisy isn't writing, she's out hiking and having fun in nature.

Written by: Daisy Anderson
Designed by: Bobbie Houser
Series Development: James Earley
Proofreader: Melissa Boyce
Educational Consultant: Marie Lemke M.Ed.
Production manager: Candice Campbell

Photographs:
t = Top, c = Center, b = Bottom, l = Left, r = Right
Alamy: Old Paper Studios: p. 6; Niday Picture Library: p. 7t; jordi clave garsot: p. 9
Library of Congress: p. 8
Shutterstock: Dancestrokes: cover, p. 1; A.Hornung: p. 4; Zack Frank: p. 5 t; Globe Turner: p. 5 b; Everett Collection: p. 7 b; Nyokki: p. 10-11; CK Foto: p. 12; Robert Bohrer: p. 13; Fernando Tatay: p. 14; Gudrun Hochmuth: p. 15; Kat Carney: p. 16; 1000Photography: p. 17; Sean R. Stubben: p. 18 tr; moosehenderson: p. 18 bl; Sundry Photography: p. 18 br; Matt Knoth: p. 19; Pascal Constantineau: p. 20; Benny Marty: p. 21; Tamara Magdyk: p. 22; Mike Ver Sprill: p. 23; Fringe78: p. 24; RomanSlavik.com: p. 25; Dudarev Mikhail: p. 26; GizaDog: p. 27; Aleksei Potov: p. 28; Meyta: p. 28 r; Nido Huebl: p. 29

Crabtree Publishing

crabtreebooks.com 800-387-7650

Printed in the U.S.A./CP2025

Published in Canada
Crabtree Publishing
616 Welland Ave.
St. Catharines, Ontario
L2M 5V6

Published in the United States
Crabtree Publishing
347 Fifth Ave
Suite 1402-145
New York, NY 10016

Library and Archives Canada Cataloguing in Publication
Available at Library and Archives Canada

Library of Congress Cataloging-in-Publication Data
Available at the Library of Congress

Hardcover: 978-1-0398-6486-3
Paperback: 978-1-0398-6555-6
Ebook (pdf): 978-1-0398-6624-9
Epub: 978-1-0398-6693-5